THE ELLIE PROJECT

A CHILDREN'S GUIDE TO BUILDING CHARACTER FROM THE FINAL WORDS OF A LOVING FATHER

Andrew B. Heard and **Bailey B. Heard**

Clovercroft Publishing

The Ellie Project: A Children's Guide to Building Character from the Final Words of a Loving Father

Published by Clovercroft Publishing, Franklin, Tennessee

Published in association with Larry Carpenter of Christian Book Services, LLC
www.christianbookservices.com

Cover and Interior Design by Suzanne Lawing

Editing by Gail Fallen

Printed in the United States of America

978-1-940262-97-0

Ellie:

You are so beautiful! I love you so much. When you read this remember God is bigger than we think. I love you and always will!

Love,

Daddy

Friends don't always look like you!

THE STORY BEHIND *THE ELLIE PROJECT*

Hi! My name is Bailey Heard. I'm Ellie's mom. I have the honor and privilege of helping to make the dream of *The Ellie Project* become a reality! This whole book started in 2012 when my husband, Andrew Heard, was diagnosed with cancer at the age of twenty-nine. This was Andrew's second battle with cancer (his first battle was when he was eighteen years old). The cancer came back eleven years later and took his life in a short ten months.

During the few months Andrew had left on this earth, he decided he wanted to leave a legacy by helping to inspire and encourage the lives of others through writing books. His book, *A Gray Faith*, was published a month before he passed away, and you are holding his second book *The Ellie Project*.

Andrew wrote *The Ellie Project* as a way to connect with our two-year-old daughter Ellie Grace. He was confined to a hospital bed in our house, so he couldn't play with her in a conventional way. He got creative and knew that she loved to draw and she loved animals, so each night she would crawl into his hospital bed and they would draw together. When Andrew was a child, he wanted to be a cartoonist, so he enjoyed drawing pictures of Ellie's favorite animals. Andrew got the idea to create a different animal for each letter in the alphabet and then he wanted to write Ellie love letters about character lessons he wanted her to know throughout her life. He was able to finish A through Z before he passed away on July 26, 2013.

I'm beyond excited to bring you this inspiring character building alphabet book. My hope is that *The Ellie Project* will help to not only teach your kids the alphabet, but will teach them character lessons that will stay with them throughout their lives. The book was written and illustrated with love from an adoring father to his daughter with the intention of connecting and encouraging her to know what truly matters in this life. These are Andrew's original drawings and writings. I hope you enjoy reading and sharing this book with the ones you love!

Blessings.

Bailey Heard

 LOWFISH

E
A
R

Ellie:

Have the hard conversations before they blow up and poke the people you love.

Love,

Daddy

ELLIE:

Courage doesn't come because you are big, strong, or without fear. Courage comes because you aren't big, you aren't strong, you do fear but you <u>don't give up!</u>

Love,

Daddy

Ellie:

The ultimate measure of a man is not where he stands in moments of comfort and convenience, but where he stands at times of challenge and controversy.

Faith gives you the strength to jump into challenge.

Love,

Daddy

EAGLE

ELLIE:

"In leadership we teach: Don't send your ducks to eagle school because it won't help. Duck finishes eagle school, sees his first rabbit, makes him a friend."

—Jim Rohn

F ROG

EAT THAT FROG!

ELLIE:

Do the hardest things first so that your days flow with the fruits of your work!

Love,
Daddy

GIRAFFE

ELLIE:

Sometimes you must look at things from a higher perspective to see what is really going on.

Love,
Daddy

WALNUT PUBLIC LIBRARY DISTRICT
Heaton & Main St.   Box 728
WALNUT, IL 61376-0728

ELLIE:

The size of your dreams and the size of your passion depend on the size of your heart!

Love,

Daddy

*I*guana

ELLIE:

Be adapative! The world changes and therefore you must! Growth is key to life, both spiritual and mental!

Love,
Daddy

J UMBO

Ellie:

Remember the elephant never forgets, so never forget that God's love is eternal. My love for you is eternal, and for eternity you will be _my_ _Ellie!_

Love,
Daddy

Ellie:

"There is no difference between a wise man and a fool when they fall in love."

-Unknown

So Ellie, be careful with your kisses, they are more powerful than you think!

Love,

Daddy

ELLIE:

As long as you are proud you cannot see God.

"A proud man is always looking down on things and people; and of course, as long as you are looking down, you cannot see something that is above you."

-C.S. Lewis, Mere Christianity

NEWFOUNDLAND

ELLIE:

"Be friendly to everyone. Those who deserve it the least need it the most."

-Bo Bennett

ODD

The male seahorse has the babies.

ELLIE:

Some things in life don't make sense, but that doesn't mean it isn't real! Accepting the impossible because it stands in front of you is faith!

Love,
Daddy

Peacock

Ellie:

The pride we have doesn't come from the outside but from the wonder of the work done on our inside!

Love,

Daddy

Q

U
A
I
L

Ellie:

A Quail is defined by the feather on its head. Find out what defines you and let that focus your life!

Love,

Daddy

Rabbit

Ellie:

Slow and steady wins the _race_! Don't let pride catch you sitting down while others pass you by.

Love,

Daddy

TURTLE

Ellie:

The turtle doesn't win with one <u>hard</u> stab, but with the steady pace of a <u>champion</u>!

Love,
Daddy

Unicorn

"Don't compare yourself with anyone in this world . . . if you do so, you are insulting yourself."

-Bill Gates

Ellie:

You aren't like anyone else because you are my daughter! Your mom and I will always believe in you!

Love,

Daddy

Vampire Bat

ELLIE:
Always remember to give life and not suck life.
Victims always see someone taking, our job is to see
where we can give!

Love,
Daddy

XENOPUS

"Don't take the casual approach to life. Casualness leads to casualties."

-Jim Rohn

ELLIE:

Be like the Xenopus and claw your way to all the best things in life!

Love,

Daddy

Y AK

ELLIE:

Remember to listen more than you speak!
Yakking only leads to trouble so hold your
tongue and listen! You will have more to give
and less people thinking you are stupid.

Love,

Daddy

ZEBRA

Ellie:

To change your stripes (who you are) you must realize that nothing is set, you can always grow and where your stripes are today is just the place you move from tomorrow.

Love,

Daddy